100 YEARS OF STYLE

BY DECADE
& DESIGNER

VOLUME 1

1900–1949

First printing

1 3 5 7 9 8 6 4 2

The Chelsea House World Wide Web address is
http://www.chelseahouse.com

Library of Congress Cataloging-in-Publication Data applied for

ISBN 0 7910 6192 2 Fashions 1900–1949 (this edition)

0 7910 6193 0 Fashions 1950–2000
0 7910 6194 9 Fashion Designers A–F
0 7910 6195 7 Fashion Designers G–M
0 7910 6196 5 Fashion Designers N–Z
0 7910 6191 4 (set)

Produced by Carlton Books
20 Mortimer Street
London W1N 7RD

Text and Design copyright © Carlton Books Limited 1999/2000

Photographs copyright © 1999 Condé Nast Publications Limited

Previous page: Giorgio Armani's understated elegance of 1996: a black
silk evening dress suspended from a neck band, sweeping to the floor.

Opposite: 'Lovely in Leather': Chanel's black leather single-breasted
fitted jacket, worn over a matching pencil skirt, 1995.

Overleaf: Gucci's Tom Ford swaps East-Coast minimalism for West-
Coast colour, splashing vibrant florals over dresses, skirts and
trousers, 1999.

100 YEARS OF STYLE

BY DECADE
& DESIGNER

Linda Watson

VOLUME 1

1900–1949

Chelsea House Publishers

PHILADELPHIA

contents

She: "Straighten your tie! Everybody's staring at you!"

Introduction

Dressing is the fourth bodily function. After breathing, eating and sleeping – and excluding a couple of delicious optional extras – one of the fundamental pleasures of the human body is to clothe it. Which makes fashion – it's closest relation – pretty important.

The history of fashion touches everyone in its orbit. It runs far, far deeper than hemlines, silhouettes and colours. It is intrinsically caught up with social mores and mood changes in everything from food to mannerisms, music to sex. It lives and exists not only as one of the most ravishing and compelling of entertainments but as the surest indicator of time. Humour has always been part of its charm.

Throughout the twentieth century, *Vogue* magazine has acted as a visual filter. Each season designers have thrown ideas into the air and *Vogue* has caught them and sprinkled them over its pages. It has always been down to the century's social animals – and significant figures – whether designs transcended history or froze in suspended animation. Diana, Princess of Wales had everything: genetic perfection, model dimensions, royal connections and the mystique of a silent-movie star. Add fashion, and you have the most photo-graphed woman on the planet.

In 1909 electricity was a new sensation, and it was shocking if a woman showed an ankle. By 1916, if she smoked in public, *Vogue* concluded, 'She must be an actress.' If she wore red lipstick, she was the next best thing to a prostitute. The wearing of a veil had orgasmic powers. Trousers were slammed as 'audacious'. If bumsters had been around, Alexander McQueen would have been locked up and labelled certifiable.

Today, following the new millennium, no one bats an eyelid if dresses skim the nipples, navels are exposed and the bottom half of the buttocks are aired to ancient relatives. Nudity – the natural conclusion – will never be in fashion not just because the weather wouldn't allow it, but because it is the only style that would put the whole industry on social security.

Ever since Eve wore a fig leaf, fashion has been associated with two things: defining sexuality and committing outrageous behaviour. Even fastenings aren't immune to this. Consider the zip – 'Zippergate' – a little metal fastening that almost brought down the president of America in 1998.

The biggest change has been in the status of the designer, who until the 1950s was considered a dictator, then a director and a suggester. Now he or she airs their opinions, controls huge empires and emblazons their name across every part of your anatomy. In turn, we want to see where they live, hear what they think, find out how they function. We sleep on their pillowcases, pull their curtains across our windows, spray ourselves with their scent: the most potent way to get style under the skin.

The fly-past of designers' behaviour throughout the last century is a seminal lesson to those who are thinking of taking up fashion design professionally. The most financially successful designers have brilliant business partners; the most creative have a single vision; the most famous are those who either have visionary tendencies or big mouths. Sometimes both. Then there are the handful of geniuses who put beauty and art before everything – and inevitably ended up with nothing: the great Orientalist, Paul Poiret, once held the fashion world in the palm of his hand; the brilliant Ossie Clark, who could cut like a dream but couldn't handle his own talent; Charles James, who was posthumously revered, but spent his declining years in New York's seedy Chelsea Hotel with sketches, toiles and an Afro wig for company. Passion and fashion – unless there's a business brain in the frame – don't mix.

Age and body shape are part of the fashion template. In 1909 the face said 20, the waist said 15, the bosom 50. Flappers started smoking furiously in an attempt to echo the streamline shape of a greyhound. By 1960 there was the ludicrous situation where women of 40-plus were dressing like 10-year-olds. A hundred years from now,

fashion historians flicking through this series, en route to a fortnight on the moon, may assume that millennium woman looked like Kate Moss. We don't.

Today, there is more choice than ever. Status symbols on every seam. We are in a world of international fashion, but the elegance on the street has gone. The skill which required, time, talent and a steady hand reached its peak of perfection in the 1950s and went rapidly downhill after the advent of television. Before 1960 women were fitted by their dressmakers. Now we make our own decisions on what size we are. Not wise. As Jean Muir once observed, 'People make pictures of themselves that other people have to look at.'

For fashion, read: prediction. In the 1920s Cecil Beaton imagined that nuns would wear cubes on their heads and brides would wear bodysuits. In the 1960s Yves Saint Laurent said he would prefer a pill to eating. He was not alone: almost everyone believed that by the year 2000 we'd be wearing spacesuits to the office and coming home to dinner with a robot.

What of the future? American minimalist Geoffrey Beene has been saying for years that 'the fundamental change will happen when the chemist meets the artist'. We already have temperature-sensitive and virtually indestructible fabrics. In the future, pundits predict clothes with in-built mobile phones; shops where we don't rifle through rails but pick prototypes, and our measurements are drawn up on a computer. No doubt, one day, someone will invent a range of skirts which have meaningful conversations with washing machines.

Designers are currently floating the idea of fashion shows on the internet. Can editors exist in a world devoid of gossip, seating arrangements and air kissing? Virtual reality in solitary confinement? Highly unlikely. For fashion is not – and never has been – about clothes. It's about people. Until genetic engineers decree otherwise. As long as the average human body is made up of four basic components – one head, two arms, two legs and fleshy undulations in the middle – fashion will continue to excite and delight within those strict, but endlessly fascinating, perimeters.

1900-09

The Vicomtesse des Touches was all in mauve mousseline de soie. Her great manteau, formed of cunning shirrs, loops and folds was lined with Liberty satin of a deeper shade. On her gloveless hands, were rings of yellow topazes. Silver shoes and silver woven stockings revealed themselves as she strolled over the grass under the bright electric lights.

Paris, ***Vogue***, 19 August 1909

The Edwardian body beautiful had rotund breasts, a handspan waist, accentuated hips and a protruding posterior. The S-bend corset (christened 'The Health Corset' without any sense of irony) convoluted the spine. Feet were squashed into minuscule shoes, hats were balanced on a concoction of pads, wigs and human hair. The female anatomy routinely stood at an angle of 33 degrees. It was the only time this century that bodies were uniformly corsetted. Fashion was a form of legalized torture. The then *Vogue* editor, Mrs Josephine Redding, a maverick figure who wore sensible shoes, no corsets and a huge hat to receive guests in bed was not amused: 'Humps,' she declared. 'Today women are covered with humps. Big humpy sleeves, humps on their hips, humps on their behinds. It's nonsense.'

By 1900 the sleeves had been deflated, whalebone corsets were intact and the eccentric Mrs Redding – who was more interested in the welfare of animals than the vagaries of skirt length – had gone to pastures new. During the *belle époque*, fashion was divided into two types of women: those who wore corsets and those who did not. The latter formed a minute proportion of free thinkers and aesthetes who embraced the principles of the Arts and

LEFT **The absurdity of huge hats and sinuous figures was relentlessly satirized, and metamorphosed into flowerpots and lampshades, 1909.**

OPPOSITE ***Vogue*'s cover of 18 March 1909 encapsulates all the elements of the Arts and Crafts movement, including rich colour and organic lines.**

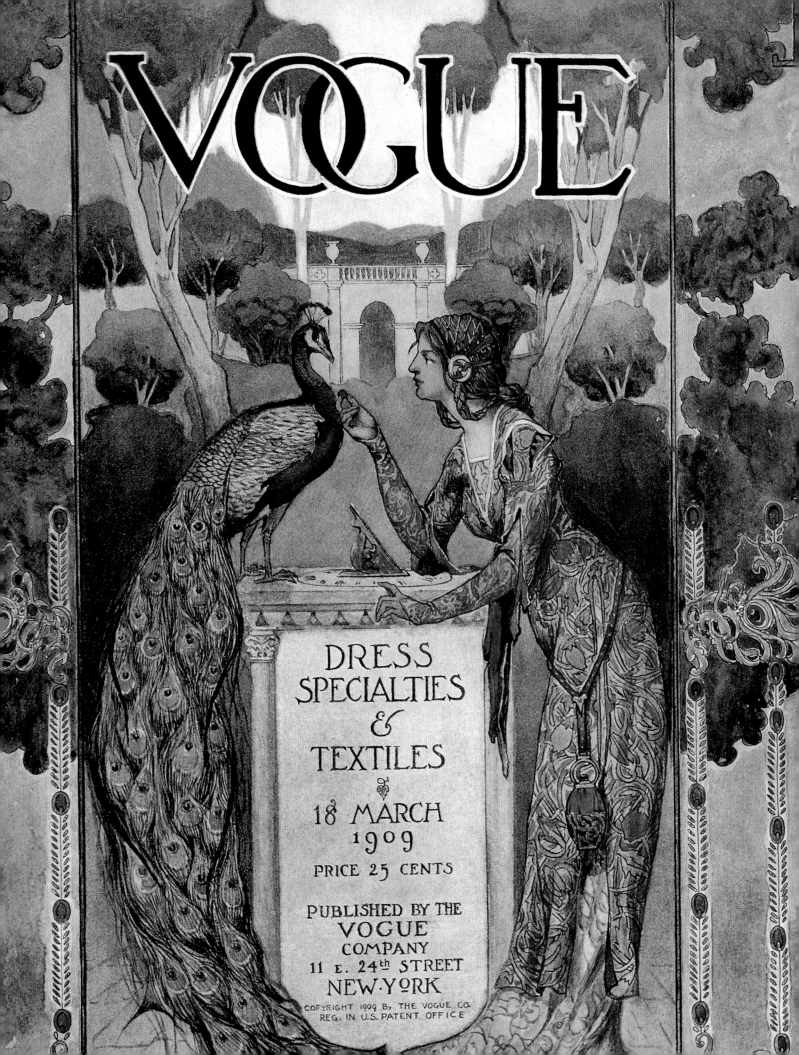

VOGUE

DRESS
SPECIALTIES
&
TEXTILES

18 MARCH
1909
PRICE 25 CENTS

PUBLISHED BY THE
VOGUE
COMPANY
11 E. 24th STREET
NEW·YORK

ABOVE **Systematic dressing for specific occasions: luncheon and reception gowns, with enormous plumed hats worn indoors, 11 February 1909.**

RIGHT **The 'new and seasonable' silhouette, in side view, was a series of undulations, curves and contortions, all held in place by one corset.**

Crafts movement and aspired to universal Empire lines. Oscar Wilde was a principal advocate. Ninety years before Women's Liberation told its followers to burn their bras, Wilde was telling his audience to eliminate their corsets.

Vogue was launched in New York on 17 December 1892 into an era of aesthetic dress reform and fashion dictatorship with an illustration of a woman walking on air and the words 'Vogue – A Debutante' on the cover. Published weekly and costing ten cents per issue, *Vogue*'s coverline cited 'Fashion, Manners, Society, The House, Literature, Art, Music, Drama' as its contents. The features extended far beyond the confines of corsetry. A popular column entitled 'Concerning Animals' carried a 'warning to flesh eaters' and a lecture on 'the gorilla, the chimpanzee and man'. Elsewhere, 'society's injustice to the child' was positioned opposite 'The Winter Mode as seen in France'. Fashion was not the main consideration. A natural reaction: when the first issue hit the newsstands, the fashion industry was in its infancy. By 1900 there was one world-famous fashion designer, no catwalks, no predictions pages and Paris was the undisputed instigator of every fashion revolution. There were only five notable names – Callot Sœurs, Madeleine Chéruit, Jacques Doucet, Jeanne Lanvin and Charles Worth, who founded his house in 1858, and made his name dressing Empress Eugénie.

by a dark-eyed beauty in the pesage', and 'an odd skirt, seen at the Paris races, [which] gave the effect of being turned upside down'.

Only a small percentage of *Vogue*'s readership had access to Paris. *Vogue*'s role was to pinpoint and popularize the look. Ready-mades – a system of mass production of clothes which later became known as 'off the peg' – had already started at the end of the nineteenth century. But this was largely confined to the most basic tailored pieces for everyday wear – the majority of fashionable women had their clothes made to measure. One section, 'Descriptions of Fashion', did exactly that. Page upon page of microscopic detail on individual garments– from colour to cut, from embellishment to button type. These were veiled instructions for dressmakers – to enable pattern-cutting – pages of fabrics shown in minute detail with information on trim, colour, texture and even length. 'Skirt and low corsage were joined by a three-inch belt of English embroidery on fine batiste. Fancy! From the shoulders, dropping to within a few inches of the belt, soft folds of satin formed the corsage below a modestie of white tulle shirred to a round yoke of embroidery.' *Vogue* not only gave its readers outlines of desirable garments, but put fashion in a social situation. 'Three Fetching Frocks seen at Monte Carlo' of 1909 evoked the atmosphere: 'Everyone streamed into the private baccarat room of the club. There, bending over a table deeply engrossed in the fate of her gold pieces, I saw a titled young New York woman. She was charming in a gown – a Chéruit, I divined – of greenish gold, embroidered filet and blue voile.' *Vogue*'s headings were plain and to the point. Notices included marriages and deaths. Advertisements listed boas and feathers, cleaners and dyers, corsets, furs, gowns and waists, hairdressing, massage, millinery and shopping commissions – a 1909 take on the personal shopper. Readers' preoccupations were defined as 'Seen in the Shops', 'Smart Fashion

Fashion movements did not spring from shows, but were publicized at the prestigious French racecourses – Longchamp, Auteuil – which were a magnet for stylish society and the Edwardian equivalent of the front row. *Vogue* turned voyeur, telling its readers what was going on, who was going where, but also – far more tantalizingly – who was wearing what. New sensations seen for the first time at the racecourses were relayed to the readers. In August 1909 *Vogue* reiterated their importance: 'At Auteuil, Chantilly and other noted French race-courses many of the newest modes are first seen in public and there frankly displayed for comment and criticism.' These included 'Moyen Âge effect in corsage and sash drapery', 'an Oriental turban worn for Limited Incomes', 'Society Snapshots' and 'Haphazard Jottings'. Dressmaking was essential. *Vogue* advertised the pneumatic dress form – inflated to the appropriate size by using a bicycle pump. *Vogue*'s pattern service started in 1899. Readers selected a garment from the issue, snipped a coupon, paid 50 cents and received a hand-cut pattern by the originator of the service, Mrs Payne. The fluctuating body shapes of a wide readership did not present a problem. 'At that time and for several years afterwards the problem of pattern sizes was simple,' reported Edna Woolman Chase, later *Vogue* editor-in-chief, in her memoirs. 'There was one – and it was a thirty-six.' As the decade progressed, *Vogue* covers, which had previously been strictly black and white, and reminiscent of the Arts and Crafts movement with woodcut borders and peacocks, changed. Colour crept in. By 1909 the *Vogue* coverline said simply, 'A Weekly Magazine of Fashion and Society'. *Vogue*'s first photographic cover showed a small black and white photograph of stylish racegoers sitting on a bench at Auteuil. With women changing their outfits up to six times per day, *Vogue* started dedicating individual issues to social occasions and specific items of dress: these included 'Southern Issue', 'Pattern Number', 'Textile and Dress Specialities', 'Millinery Number', 'Corset and Lingerie', 'Announcements of Autumn Fashion'

LEFT By 1909 Orientalism was creeping in. Turbans were considered risqué and the body was beginning to strike a new pose: standing up straight.

BELOW *Vogue*'s first photographic scene, 8 July 1909, is of elegantly turned-out women at the French races, putting fashion in a social setting.

and even an 'Outing Number', which discussed the delights of house-boating, gymkhana games and canoe picnics.

Millinery was a big issue. As the silhouette grew slimmer and less complicated, hats were growing ever more elaborate and out of control. Even though *Vogue* was advocating the look, caricaturists were given free reign to highlight the absurdity of enormous hats, turning them into gigantic lampshades, flowerpots, cages and cabbages. 'Paris is laughing heartily over our contemporary freaks of fashion,' reported *Vogue* in July 1909. 'They are the subject of daily jokes in the papers and have inspired the comic artistry of the Boulevards in the form of post cards and toys.'

As the hats expanded, so too did the hair. The beauty ideal was one of fresh complexion. Tightly corsetted from armpit to thigh, collars

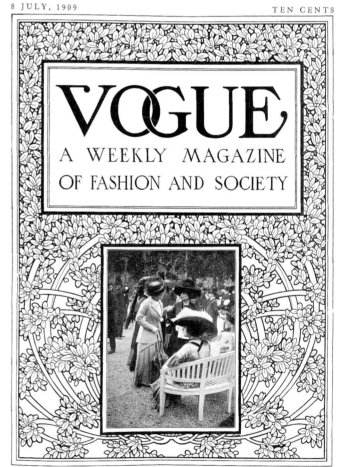

8 JULY, 1909   TEN CENTS

VOGUE
A WEEKLY MAGAZINE OF FASHION AND SOCIETY

THE VOGUE COMPANY 11 EAST 24TH STREET NEW YORK CITY
VOL. XXXIV, No. II   Copyright, 1909, By The Vogue Company   Reg. in U. S. Patent Office   WHOLE NUMBER 865

featherboned to the chin, women were barely able to sit down – let alone take a brisk walk in the park. Instead, a rosy-cheeked look was achieved by stimulating the skin electronically. *Vogue* readers could try the Davis electric medical battery, which 'causes rich red blood to go leaping, bounding and tingling through the body. Recommended for chronic headaches and worn-out systems. Nothing like it.'

With a corset that was purporting ample breasts and a tiny waist, *Vogue* advertisements reveal the method and madness of simulating roundness in one area and starvation in another. There was no mention of eating less. Exercise was out of the question. Fashionable beauty aids included Dr Walter's medicated rubber reducing corset, Edna hip confiner or Louisenbad reduction salts which claimed to eliminate inches through evaporation. Poise was an important consideration. Instruction was given on how to sit, with *Vogue* stating: 'The manner in which women sit down in their present-day gowns deserves to be an object of special study on the part of all persons.'

Vogue's feature writers mixed social issues with fashion observations. *Vogue*'s Monte Carlo correspondent wrote a section between 'Parasols Very Lovely' and 'Shocking Indifference to Anguish' on the fashionable pursuit of pigeon shooting: 'Wavering a moment, it falls to earth; while still fluttering, a dog retrieves it, and the sport goes on. Passing on the beautiful terrace above this slaughter-ground with averted eyes, I noticed a silk coat of quite a new cut.'

Edwardian dressing was exhausting and confined to strict rules of propriety. *Vogue* gave suggestions for every occasion: ravishing carriage cloaks, handsome winter toilettes for 'Horse Show Wear', 'Pretty Dust Coats' for the traveller, club gowns for morning and afternoon. Mourning dress had specific and particular constraints. *Vogue* advised a black crepe veil worn over the face for six months, and back from the face for 12 months or two years – 'longer if one wishes'. *Vogue* readers had been prised from the roulette tables and encouraged to take part in country pursuits. Hats started to shrink in size. Practicality started to creep into *Vogue*'s vocabulary. Automobiles – by now so popular that models were being designed specifically for women – demanded a different dress code and accompanying accessories. Coats which had been extremely tight-fitting were now 'very baggy and loose ... across the bust and chest'. Wind cuffs were included to keep the wrists and arms dry. An adjustable motor cap, in the form of a knitted veil, came in 'pure silk with a wee invisible fuzz on the surface that makes it impossible for dust to penetrate to the face or hair'. Accessories included a folding

footstool, goggles, touring bags and gloves. *Vogue* advised investing in a crystal vase and yellow chrysanthemums: 'a few of these, bunching with red, give a lively bunch of colour as the cars whiz by'.

By 1909 *Vogue* was more concerned with highlighting movements than protecting its readers from fashion faux pas. Sportswear was running parallel to the Paris collections. By the end of the decade, designers who had been recognizable only by their label started to air their views. Paul Poiret, a high-profile *enfant terrible* who made his name dressing Mrs Asquith, the British prime minister's wife, was asked about his 'Ideals of Elegance in Dress'. This was *Vogue*'s first designer interview. 'There are in Paris at the present time only ten entities, ten silhouettes – no more; that is to say ten categories under which nearly all women are to be ranked. The ones who escape this classification are, in my opinion, the only *élégantes* worthy of the name,' said Poiret, who upended the fashion world by reviving Orientalism, drawing the Directoire line and instigating the return of the natural figure. Mariano Fortuny took the idea of freedom to extremes, patenting a silk pleated tube in 1908. But it was Poiret's Orientalism, coinciding with the arrival of the Ballet Russes, which captured the world's imagination. Poiret was advocating individuality. 'I can hardly repress a shrug of the shoulders when I hear someone ask, at the beginning of Summer: What will be the fashionable colour? For the love of the *Bon Dieu*, I say, Madame, choose yourself the form and colour of your clothes.' By the end of the decade, women were standing up straight.

RIGHT Fashion's first *enfant terrible*, Paul Poiret, changed the world with his radical ideas, love of Empire lines and insistence on eliminating the corset. The illustration is drawn by his 'artistic collaborateur', Paul Iribe.

1910–19

They really shouldn't allow a veil like this. All the men should rise in a body and make it a law for any woman to be so attractive. It's just a frill of black lace, but it has been attached to the inside of the hat, just where the crown rests on the head. It really should be stopped – men have a hard enough time in this world as it is.

Makers of Mystery, *Vogue*, early December 1917

The ankle had been seen, corsets were sliding down a few inches and in April 1911 *Vogue* started talking about trousers. Throwing adjectives into the air, *Vogue* wondered whether they were 'audacious' and 'sensational', or 'demure' and 'coquettish', then threw down the gauntlet: 'HAS PARIS OVER-REACHED HERSELF IN HER LATEST DIVERTING SENSATION?' Even the designers – who floated the idea in the first place – were in shock. *Vogue* interviewed Worth in his salon on rue de la Paix about the possibility of women wearing trousers – the 1911 version consisted of voluminous pantaloons concealed beneath a long skirt. Would they become covetable? 'Yes, certainly they will,' declared Worth, 'they will accept it because it is vulgar, ugly and wicked – those reasons insure the success of any article of feminine wear! The world has gone mad! All conversation concentrates itself on this most detestable garment!' Would Worth be showing them? 'I shall not endorse it, Madame; but if they demand it, they must have it.'

Within a decade, designers were producing clothes that were kick-started by the new issues of practicality and necessity. In an age of static beauty, activity had been

LEFT **A glimpse of a trouser leg, shown by Worth in 1911, was enough to shock fashion pundits. Earliest versions were Oriental pantaloons worn under side-slit skirts.**

OPPOSITE **By 1913 a new silhouette, created by Paul Poiret, had revolutionized fashion, comprising hobble skirt, smaller hat and free-flowing figure.**

RIGHT **Mrs Benjamin S Guinness, who brought the first Pekinese to America, photographed with Wung Tung in 1911. Miniature** **dogs were the new must-have: 'the smaller the dog the more valuable, best weight under eight pounds', decreed** *Vogue.*

unthinkable. Now sportswear was gaining momentum. In January 1910 *Vogue* featured 'The Motor Girl' on its cover and inside debated the decline of the horse. Cycling, skiing, golfing and fishing were popular, as were yachting and tennis. 'Motoring is now so much a part of everyday life that one thinks nothing of a forty-mile run to polo or the races and back,' reported *Vogue* in 1911, 'but it is quite necessary to be prepared with suitable wraps, hats and veils to enjoy the trip comfortably and to be ready to start on a minute's notice.'

Although practicality was now part of *Vogue*'s vocabulary, there was still room for the frivolous and fanciful. *Vogue* carried advertisements for the tango brassiere and tango shoe, offsetting informative pieces on sports attire against flimsier features on 'Fashions and Foibles of Parisiennes', 'Boudoir Intimacies', 'Trivialities of the Summer Stage' and even 'Etiquette at Buckingham Palace', an in-depth analysis of royal protocol for New Yorkers who might find themselves taking tea with King Edward VII.

Paul Poiret invented the hobble skirt and, by his own admission, transferred restriction from one area to another. 'Like all great revolutions, that one had been made in the name of Liberty – to give free play to the abdomen,' he later stated in his biography

OPPOSITE TOP Last bastion of the *belle époque* – flyaway hats, here drawn by *Vogue*'s caricaturist in 1917 and described as 'freak' and 'aeroplanitory'.

RIGHT A high priestess of clothes, Lady Duff Gordon, alias 'Lucile', was advocating Empire lines. Her sister was the radical novelist and original It Girl, Elinor Glyn.

FAR RIGHT Some Parisians were already ahead of their time, wearing tight hobble skirts, snug-fitting hats, and accompanied by lean dogs – a look which was to characterize the 1920s.

My First Fifty Years (1931). 'It was equally in the name of Liberty that I proclaimed the fall of the corset and the adoption of the brassiere which, since then, has won the day. Yes, I freed the bust, but I shackled the legs. Everyone wore the tight skirt.'

Poiret continued to set the standard, flying in the face of every preconceived idea, mesmerizing the world with his ability to translate the most opulent Orientalism into wearable works of art. In 1912 he designed fur-trimmed lampshade tunics for a ballet, *Le Minaret*. The following year he translated this outlandish theatrical idea into his collection. Its popularity was assured when Madame Georgette, a high-profile Parisian *vendeuse*, wore Poiret's invention at The Drags.

Impeccably bred dogs in exclusive varieties were the new fashion accessory. 'The Pekingese now Claims to be the Smartest Dog in Dogdom,' stated *Vogue* in 1911, reporting on a show in the ballroom of the Plaza Hotel, where the breed was launched. Preferred pedigrees included the Pekingese, Boston bull, Maltese terrier, Yorkshire terrier, French bull terrier – 'the height of fashion a few seasons ago' – and English spaniel – 'in dainty sizes which fit snugly under the arm'. *Vogue* published portraits of owners and their pets – appropriately named Lady Prim, Gloriette Smith and champion English spaniel, Mamselle Fifi.

Parisian designers no longer expected customers to come to them; instead they crossed the Atlantic with samples from their latest collections. Paul Poiret, a supreme public relations strategist, was already well known in America, travelling there with his wife Denise, who acted as muse and walking advertisement. Lady Duff Gordon, sister to novelist Elinor Glyn, designed under the label 'Lucile' and was an aristocratic Englishwoman who built her look on Empire lines and illusions of languor. Claiming to be 'the greatest living creator of fashions', and already established in Paris, Lady Duff Gordon stormed New York, arriving in Murray Hill and inviting the smart set to inspect her wares. Designers had been christening their gowns for decades, but Lucile went into romantic raptures, with names such as 'Hesitate no Longer', 'His Lullaby' and 'Why so Lonely?'.

For centuries, fashion followed a single line; now it was careering in different directions. Innovations no longer took years to filter through; radical changes occurred seasonally. By 1913 collections were reported in their correct timescale, and fashion was considered a dictator, residing in Paris and often out of control. In September 1913 *Vogue* instilled the fear factor into its fashion pages, announcing 'The Tyranny

of the Neck Frill' and 'The Tyrannizing Flounce', while Paris was ominously described as 'The City which must be Obeyed'. By October, *Vogue* felt designers were starting to believe their own publicity, and that egos needed to be suppressed: 'Every designer is a superman, a Nietzsche of the world, insistent that his own inflated egoism direct the trend of fashion. They stand in their booths in *Vanity Fair*, each crying his wares, each announcing that there is but one Mode and that he is its Prophet.'

Paris retaliated by resorting to shock tactics. In December 1913 *Vogue* reported Lucile's show. She had explored the American market and was no longer into neoclassical lines. Instead, she echoed Paul Poiret's Minaret silhouette, turning to flaring tunics and tango frocks with matching tango hair. *Vogue* was pleasantly surprised: 'Some of them wore green hair, some red hair, and some blue hair! Until one sees it, one has no idea how very chic blue hair can be. A violet frock demanded violet hair – of course

BELOW **Paul Poiret's Minaret tunics were both radical and dramatic, and combined the line of the hobble skirt with the theatricality of the crinoline, 1913.**

it did, what could be more natural – but with a green frock one would not think of combining green hair – why, red hair, of course, with a green frock!'

Despite being taken with the odd eccentricity, *Vogue* announced: '1913 will go down in history as the year when couturiers showed everything from fig leaves to hoop skirts, if one may dignify by the term "fig leaves" the very flimsy, transparent creations which are so décolleté and so split that a covering they certainly are not.' In the same year a new corset, 'The Debutante Slouch', was introduced, made from a combination of elastic and tricot. *Vogue* announced its first lingerie number in December, and the following May made a point of expressing its amazement at the newest sartorial affrontery – 'DÉCOLLETÉ IN BROAD DAYLIGHT?' On the edge of indecency, designers were brought back to earth.

The First World War broke out. In October 1914 *Vogue* reported, 'Paris is in a state of siege, but flags are fluttering gaily on all sides just as if the city were in gala dress to welcome a royal guest. But today Paris is not preparing to welcome a monarch – but to keep one out.' Paul Poiret, still under 40 years old, was among the first reservists to be called up to the French infantry. 'The Latest, perhaps the Last, Paris Fashions,' said *Vogue*, followed by, 'Paris is as arid of fashion material as the desert of Sahara according to one of *Vogue*'s Parisian artists, who arrived in New York recently.'

Couturiers carried on, but by November 1915, fearing isolation from Paris and knowing that there was no American fashion industry, *Vogue* set up a fund to help. A fashion fête of Le Syndicat de Défense de la Grande Couture Française, of which Poiret was the president, took place at the Ritz-Carlton hotel to benefit the widows and orphans of French soldiers.

When British *Vogue* was launched, on 15 September 1916, with 'The Forecast of Autumn Fashions' on the cover, *Vogue* switched its emphasis from reporting and discussing, to predicting and defining. 'Paris lifts ever so little the ban on gaiety,' reported *Vogue* in November 1916. 'Surprising things are likely to happen almost every day in Paris. One sees women clad in brilliant red when they should never come even within shopping distance of red material. One sees other women swathed to the very chin in green when green is the one colour that gives them the appearance of being visited with a severe attack of *mal de mer*.' In April 1917 'Vogue Points' predicted the most important looks of the next decade. First, the cloche hat 'is having an enormous vogue in Paris, where for months we have been devoted to the Russian turban. Next, trousers 'If womankind once gets over the stile and into the pantalon will she care to climb back and into the prosaic skirt?' The following year, tapering skirts were given a trouser effect, gathered in the centre and clinging at the ankles. *Vogue* announced that the potato was no longer fashionable. By the victory spring of 1919, Paris reverted to the Tanagra silhouette, skirts were shorter than ever and silk jersey was the new sensation. Hair was now cut to the nape of the neck and smoking in public was still regarded as scandalous. *Vogue* observed: 'It wasn't so very long ago when, if a woman smoked in a London hotel, people gazed at her in wide-eyed wonder and murmured apologetically, "She must be an actress."'

While Britain reeled from the emotional and economic consequences of war, androgynous dressing was on the threshold. Fashion had reached a point of no return: 'He who Returns from the War May Find that the Only Profession Left him is that of a Female Impersonator', stated the headline in *Vogue*, August 1919. It was positioned above a feature discussing role reversal by Dorothy Parker, in which she said: 'The style in heroines has changed completely. In fact, the style in all women has changed. It is all directly due to the war – the war, which started so many things that it couldn't possibly finish.'

1920–29

The Vamp: A very special brand. You propose to her by telephone and marry her by wireless. You do not make a home and lead her in, but mix a cocktail and take her out. She will probably demand a divorce on the grounds of incompatibility of dance steps. Only suitable for millionaires.

The Woman of Your Choice, *Vogue*, early November 1923

The 1920s were the age of abbreviation – or as *Vogue* succinctly put it in 1924: 'This is the period of short skirts, shirt shrift, short credit and short names. How could one "make an effect" if one answered to the name of Tots, or Marg or Babs, or Sibbie?' The new signatures – straight lines, bobbed hair, flat breasts, boyish bodies – became the template for a decade of decadence. Fashion was no longer the sum of the parts, but a Rubik cube with endless permutations. The distasteful turned tasteful: Russian water-rat fur was used as trimming; a fan made from vulture feathers was dipped in gold. As thin equalled chic, the preferred pet of the time became a greyhound.

Women were now borrowing cufflinks and brandishing cigarette holders, but still wondering whether to bare their arms in daylight. *Vogue* covers reflected their dilemma. In January 1920 the magazine's cover was a Dickensian figure walking through a snowstorm with a plum pudding under her arm. By December of that year she had metamorphosed into a fully-fledged vamp, complete with a plunging bare-back dress and long, lacquered talons. The beautifully illustrated covers continued to flick backwards and forwards in time. No longer hesitant and monotone, editorial was spiced with humour and comment, analysis and predictions. Fashion had an esoteric edge; *Vogue* discussed 'Fashions of the Mind'.

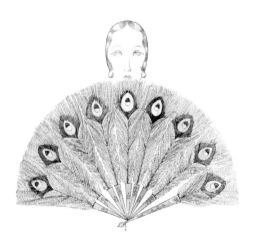

LEFT **The fan was the last bastion of flirtation: this 'gay fan of spreading peacock feathers' was worn with heavy eyelids and a shingle haircut, 1924.**

OPPOSITE **The deliciously sexy vamp: with long, red lacquered talons, visible make-up and a bare shoulder – a revolutionary *Vogue* cover in December 1921.**

VOGUE

Late December 1921

CONDÉ NAST & CO LTD
LONDON

One Shilling & Six Pence Net

Aldous Huxley remembered 'Fashions in Love', Léon Bakst analysed the slim silhouette. Style was defined with absolute precision. 'What the Germans call *Zeitgeist*, I prefer to call fashion,' said *Vogue*. 'It's a prettier word.'

The term 'Mode' still denoted authority, but the favourite expression on the tip of everyone's tongue was 'modern'. Aldous Huxley wrote an essay on 'The Vulgarity of Modern Life'; the beauty pages talked about 'Chic and ultramodern hair'. In 1929 the Duchesse D'Ayen stated that, 'The modern ideal of loveliness is not a passive one. Statuesque beauty is out of date.'

Vogue featured its first fashion shoot, 'A Group of Paris Frocks that Posed for *Vogue*', in November 1920. Fashion was now as much about the basic ingredients – fabric and colour, length and shape – as poise and attitude. In 1922 *Vogue* spoke out: 'It is the fashionable – no matter how snobbish one feels in saying it – who set the fashion. The larger their number, the deeper their pockets.' International socialites were described and drawn in suspended animation by *Vogue*'s star photographer, writer and social butterfly, Cecil Beaton. He recalled Lady Diana Cooper's 'expression of mad surprise in her sky-blue eyes', heralded Edith Sitwell as 'a Gothic Madonna of unparalleled beauty', and gleefully related a tale of a private party in 1928 where George Gershwin sang 'S'wonderful! S'marvellous!' for the first time, noting a Miss Mary Baker – 'the shy bride of Chicago' – as having 'the smallest hands and feet in the world'. The freedom to sit and stand at whim was a novelty. Simplicity was a modern concept, and fashion was mesmerized by it. In 1920 there were rumours of a renaissance of the crinoline and pannier.

One year on, the notion was dismissed as ridiculous: 'Slip-on frocks, chemise frocks, and models of straight lines, carefully adjusted to each individual figure, prove that the vogue for simplicity will continue.' The 'new chemise frock' was not made up – as it had been originally – of rectangles and squares, but now slightly shaped at the shoulder and virtually identical, back and front. By 1923 the silhouette had turned into a tube.

The concept of the female designer was already firmly established. Coco Chanel had been admired for her use of jersey and a specially woven knit, kasha, during the 1910s, but by the 1920s she had come into her own. Madeleine Chéruit and Madeleine Vionnet, whose uncomplicated lines were nothing short of revolutionary, 'returned to the simple, absolutely straight frock which looks like a uniform of some religious order, save as to length', said *Vogue*. Two years previously, Vionnet caused a sensation by producing a gown that 'not only was not lined, but had not even a

LEFT **Smoking, which had been a strictly private pleasure in the 1910s, was a flappers' delight. It conveniently kept one's weight in check.**

ABOVE **Greyhounds, lean and fast – echoing the shape of their owners – appeared regularly. They later became a symbol of the British working classes.**

real fastening'. With fashion literacy in its infancy, readers still
found it difficult to differentiate between designers. In January
1923 *Vogue* decided to run a prize competition to identify the
works of 12 famous designers, including Jean Patou, Paul Poiret,
Jeanne Lanvin, Jacques Doucet and Charles Worth. Each garment
was illustrated and clues were given in the form of a 'problem
play'. The first prize was a dress allowance of 100 guineas.

The competition was one of the few occasions when
cash was mentioned. Prices were never printed in *Vogue*;
economy was a dirty word. *Vogue* called the financially
disadvantaged the '*nouvelle pauvre*'. The issue of purse-
tightening was handled with absolute tact and diplomacy.
'A limited income wardrobe is like a cable,' announced *Vogue*.
'It must say what it has to say in a few words, with decision
and clarity. And the woman who achieves it must know what
to eliminate and when to say "stop".'

Elegant accessories – called the 'cleverly chosen etceteras' –
provided a frisson of excitement. There were feathered fans for
flirting, cigarette holders for smouldering. Optional extras
included huge plumes, long strands of pearls, row upon row
of plain bracelets and enormous single pear-shaped stones.
Evening scarves were a new sensation; at first draped
diagonally across the body, later knotted around the neck,

and made from silk, satin or a combination of leopardskin and
monkey fur. Stockings were universally neutral, but analysed in-
depth were four shades of grey, six shades of beige and three
types of heel detail.

In the same way as the sportswear revolution was responsible
for deconstructing corsets, fashion movements of the 1920s were
sparked by social situations. Trousers had come in through the
back door. In 1922 Paul Poiret showed pyjamas as 'original attire
for the hours of deshabille'. By 1924, when *Vogue* announced
'Pyjamas become matters of vivid importance', it was time to put
the cards on the table. '*Vogue* is not over-emphasizing a fancy of
the hour, but it is giving fair notice to a new mode that is starting
on a long career. The pyjama is not an amusing novelty; it has

The simple frock.   *The suit & blouse.*   *The coat-wrap.*   *The evening frock.*   *The chameleon gown.*   *The smart cape.*

become an essential part of the smart woman's wardrobe.' *Vogue* pinpointed three variations: sleeping pyjamas – 'a lovely, boyish thing of washing silk or crepe de Chine'; lounging pyjamas – 'when informal entertainments and masquerades are the order of the day'; and beach pyjamas – 'usually of gay printed cretonne, often worn with bright rubber wristlets to keep the sleeves in place when one loiters on the sand'. The bathing suit was no longer a useless *objet d'art*, but made from sea-friendly taffeta, Milanese silk or striped crepe de Chine. Stretch fabric was risqué. 'The newest thing for the sea is a jersey bathing-suit,' said *Vogue* in January 1924, 'as near a maillot as the unwritten law will permit.'

By 1926 genders were bending. Androgynous phrases – 'The Garçonne frock' and 'boyish bob' – slipped into the fashion curriculum. Women were not simply adopting male attire; they had actively invaded their territory. 'The Modern Rosalind – Notes on the Increasing Feminine Tendency to Borrow Men's Fashion' observed how 'the hosiers that was once a sanctum for the masculine shopper is now a battleground for women, while mere man cringes on the threshold'. Argument was provoked when Otto Weininger, a psychologist, pronounced that male and female were 'imaginary extremes rather than actual beings'. He then flicked from theory to hard fact: 'Women do the same work as men and play the same games. And until

ABOVE 'Evening wraps of brilliant tissue' – Jeanne Paquin's cloak of gold tissue and sable velvet summed up the unrestrained opulence of the 1920s.

RIGHT Midway through the 1920s, hemlines were shrinking to new heights – showing both the ankle and calf, as exemplified here by Jeanne Lanvin's 'graceful simplicity'.

they cease doing so the present tendency in their clothes is likely to continue. You cannot drive a Rolls Royce in a Gainsborough hat, amputate a limb in a crinoline, or play polo in stays.'

Women's wardrobes, once governed by strict rules of propriety, were now divided by timetables. They were unsure about what to wear in front of a typewriter. 'A Guide to Chic for the Businesswoman', suggested blending into the background with sombre colours and plain fabrics, and advised absolute caution when crossing the line between social and working hours: 'We must stoutly protest that the sport, garden party or reception dress is out of place in the shop or office. Short sleeves do not look well for such wear, ever. Elbow-length is permissible, but the really short sleeve is bad form and the sleeveless street gown is unspeakably vulgar.'

Hats echoed the shape of hair, which started the decade as a simple bob and turned, by 1923, into an undulated version called the shingle. Tongue firmly in cheek, *Vogue* imbued hats with cosmic importance, discussed the trials and tribulations of wearing silk stockings and advised that, 'The wearer must be treated like an odalisque and personally removed from the horizontal to the perpendicular.' Wrinkles could be dealt with by sticking plasters put in the appropriate place, 'particularly during moments of intense concentration'. In 1927 *Vogue* stated 'How demode it is to look chilly!' while identifying 'A Complete Set of Flappers' – six characters including 'The Go-getter': 'Scientists say this type is a cross between a standard vampire and a standard vacuum cleaner.'

By 1926 couturiers no longer concentrated solely on clothes. *Vogue* described 'The Perfume of the Couture', pointing out that Worth, the Callot Sœurs, Lucien Lelong and Poiret preferred intriguing titles, while Coco Chanel and Edward Molyneux adopted 'this restrained and cryptic method' of numbers for the fragrances they developed. Jean Patou produced three scents – one for blondes, one for brunettes and one for auburn-haired women.

Chanel opened her first London outlet in November 1927 and *Vogue* paid her the ultimate compliment: 'Mademoiselle

Chanel's dresses are peculiarly free from mistakes, either in taste or execution.'

In October 1928 the cocktail of the moment was made of Dubonnet and gin – 'half and half and shaken very cold'. *Vogue* declared 'the death of uniformity'. The art of luxury was never more mouthwatering: gold lamé over lace, over crepe satin; a brown velvet coat, with an inner casing of peach satin *fulgrante*, and an evening shoe constructed from silver tissue flecked with gold. Suntanning was chic and social values had changed so much that *Vogue* suggested 'The Dress for the Second Marriage'.

On the brink of a new decade, Aldous Huxley asked, 'Where are the Movies Moving?' and explored the extraordinary potential of cinema. He wrote: 'On the screen, miracles are easily performed; the most incongruous ideas can be arbitrarily associated, the limitations of time and space are largely ignored.' For the first time, cinema could be seen and heard. What no one could foresee was the phenomenal effect that movies with speech would have on fashion.

ABOVE **The Flapper: a good-time girl. 'Annabel is one of those little devils who starts out being the life of the party and is almost the death of it.'**

RIGHT **Chanel's 'sports ensemble' jersey sweater and wraparound skirt, 1928. Chanel was the first designer to show sportswear in a contemporary setting.**

reported on the Paris collections, carried sketches of Greta Garbo's latest film costumes, and pinpointed the movers and shakers of the movie business. Paris was working on a seasonal timescale, Hollywood was years in advance; Paris was inspired by technique and tradition, Hollywood by scripts and screen beauties. Both worked on the principles of illusion.

Parisian designers quickly realized that film would be the future of fashion. In 1930 Coco Chanel signed a contract with Samuel Goldwyn to design costumes for the stars of United Artists. The following year she embarked on her first screen collaboration, designing gowns for Gloria Swanson in *Tonight or Never* (1931). Elsa Schiaparelli, although on the periphery of the industry since the early 1920s, became the new star of Paris. Launching a counterattack to Hollywood's populist appeal, she exploited her affinity with the surrealist movement – a circle of artists and writers who worked on Freudian principles – and put a new slant on Parisian tradition. The Paris stalwarts – Madeleine Vionnet, Jean Patou, Augustabernard, Edward Molyneux, Jeanne Lanvin – all continued to produce collections of unbelievable complexity, mixing knotting and draping. In 1931 Mainbocher, a former editor of French *Vogue*, made his debut with a silhouette of fitted tunic and flaring petal shapes called Le Douze.

As cinema audiences grew and the screen became more powerful than the salon, Paris began to steer its own course. What Hollywood could do with film, Paris could match in technical brilliance. Not content with drawing seams of the most mind-boggling variety, Patou and Augustabernard experimented with spiral wrapping running from the knee to the shoulder. The concept of fantasy created by cameras and lighting was not, of course, new; fashion shoots pre-dated the 'talkies'. *Vogue*'s 'Paris Fashions as Seen by the Camera' explored the tenuous link between Hollywood glamour and the mystique of a fashion

ABOVE **'Suits to dine in'**, *Vogue*'s **masculine look of 1935, took all the elements of a man's tuxedo and toreador, and threw in a few curves.**

RIGHT **Charles James, a genius of cut and construction, was formulating pure lines and stark shapes in 1936, as seen here with his 'dead white slipper satin evening coat'.**

RIGHT **Surrealist tendencies had knocked the ability to shock.** *Dope for Debs* **illustration of 1936, showed surrealism taken to ridiculous lengths.**

She: 'Straighten your tie! Everybody's staring at you!'

VOGUE 75

shoot, featuring photographer Baron George Hoyningen-Huene and showing gowns by Patou and Vionnet. 'The great studio is in semi-darkness. Huge shapes stand out of the gloom, the outline of machinery. A tall silver screen gives off a ghostly radiance. We are in one of the greatest fashion photograph studios in the world.'

Paris and Hollywood unanimously agreed on one point: the exaggerated shoulder. Initially called the 'coat-hanger silhouette' for obvious reasons, by 1933 shoulders came in infinite varieties. There was Elsa Schiaparelli's Pagoda shoulder line, Augustabernard's shoulder flares, the square shoulder and layers of flaring shoulder tabs. Height – 'the effect of bulk which is so chic' – was added to frame the face in the form of high collars, or scarves of silver fox. By August of the same year the shoulder had gone as far as the camera would allow, and was sharply pulled back to reality. 'Paris lost its head, its heart, its judgement on shoulder exaggeration, on tulle and sleeves, on organzas, on ruffles, on sings. Paris grew sentimental. The story now will be the neck and bosom.' The emphasis switched from shoulder width to anatomical elongation by October: 'A dress starts as soon as possible, next to the chin, catches you at the throat, and leaves you gasping in so many new ways. Vionnet thought of it first.' In December *Vogue* wrote: 'There are ninety-nine neat, throat-hugging, monastic necklines. The hundredth – a dramatic exception – plunges down to the lungs. It isn't a freakish, eccentric thing. Far from it. The story goes round that the play *The Six Wives of Henry VIII* is responsible for this poitrine-exposing trend.'

Innovations in proportion were equalled by inventions in fastenings: Schiaparelli understood the novelty value of buttons, turning them into acrobats and lovebirds. The zip fastener was invented. What started out on handbags was soon to be found in every woman's wardrobe: 'Nowadays we pack so many activities into twenty-four hours that the buttons or hooks which hold the fitted line of our clothes take precious minutes to do up. This is where Lightening fasteners come in.'

Pre- 'talkies', Hollywood had been a cloistered world where clothes had limited influence beyond the confines of the film studio. Costume was defined by script and historical context, which begged the question: 'Does Hollywood Create?' Carefully giving credit where it was due, *Vogue* asked, 'Does the new, enlightened, smart Hollywood originate its own fashions? Does it come out with brand-new ideas that never saw Paris? Or is it simply the most

perfect visual medium for the exploitation of fashion that ever existed?' *Vogue* analysed individual scenarios: Greta Garbo's hair; the famous feather boas of Marlene Dietrich in *Morocco* (1930); Dietrich's ruff of cock feathers in *Shanghai Express* (1932). 'Today, every smart woman has a feather ruff or boa. Score Hollywood 2, Paris 0.' *Vogue* continued to play ping pong: 'Paris definitely had a feeling for the masculinized look about the time *Mata Hari* [1931] came out. Paris showed little pill-box hats about the time of the premiere of *Grand Hotel* [1932]. Evening dresses with high necks in front began so quietly that it is hard to trace the exact birth.' False eyelashes, originally used only by make-up artists, arrived in England.

Exaggeration continued, but in 1934 the emphasis switched from the shoulder to the sleeve. By December Schiaparelli had eclipsed Paris with her use of rayon tulle, which she called 'Cosmic', along with Rhodophane fabric, which looked exactly like glass. *Vogue* showed some of its uses on models – 'Lest you think that it is something only a cinema queen might wear.'

Hats shrank, hair had uplift. *Vogue* stated the two were still inseparable. 'Every woman has an immoderate passion for hats. She can't have too many – do you remember how young Antonia in *The Constant Nymph* [1933] put eight hats on her trousseau list and no underclothes?' The world's fascination with celebrity was set in stone. An 'incomparable' Marlene Dietrich posed in dresses designed by Travis Banton at Paramount, including a froufrou of black tulle. In the same issue *Vogue* proclaimed, 'The two opposing schools of decoration, the Great Baroque and the Starkly Simple, seem to have met at last.' *Vogue* equated fashion design to architecture: 'The era of the dressmaker, all bits and pieces and complicated seaming, gives place to that of the mathematician and architect.' A Harrow-educated Anglo-American based in

Monkey-fur melodrama for Marlene Dietrich. Reboux's hat and scarf (Pissot and Pavy)

Mummy Dresses by Paquin completely muffle you; elastic velvet lets you walk

OPPOSITE **Lucien Lelong's Robin Hood red-and-green wraps and make-up incorporated surrealist elements, with bizarre eyes and lips, and perplexing perspectives.**

RIGHT **The Honourable Mrs Reginald Fellowes wears Elsa Schiaparelli's sequinned breast-plate, photographed by Cecil Beaton. Schiaparelli enjoyed a meteoric rise in the 1930s.**

Chicago, Charles James was by now a celebrated couturier, making his mark on London. James was an undisputed master of surface austerity and intricate infrastructure; in October 1936 a cavalcade of his capes and coats appeared in Harrods' windows.

Masculine influence filtered through to Paris. The dinner suit was 'the big news in every collection – nothing in fashion is newer'. The surrealist movement influenced fashion shoots. In 1936 dresses by Robert Piguet and Elsa Schiaparelli were seen in a barren landscape – 'Rope, hurtling out of oblivion, surrealist-fashion; spring-coiling over a purple satin dress, incredibly straight, clenched with a metal zip.' On 11 June 1936 London opened its first International Surrealist Exhibition. In January 1937 *Vogue* published a portrait of Salvadore Dalí opposite an explanation of a movement which had, by now, been seen and heard: 'A Surrealist is a man who likes to dress like a fencer, but does not fence; a Surrealist is also a man who likes to wear a diving suit, but does not dive. Mr Dalí recently delivered a speech in London dressed in a diving suit (he nearly smothered to death because someone forgot to open the air-valve).'

Vogue continued to feature film stars in fashion settings. In 1937 Ginger Rogers floated across the pages of *Vogue* in swathes of chiffon. Hollywood designer Gilbert Adrian, working at Metro-Goldwyn-Mayer, described dressing Greta Garbo for *Camille* (1937) and Norma Shearer in *Marie Antoinette* (1938). By the time *Gone with the Wind* (1939) preoccupied the gossip columnists, film fashion had moved from slink fit to crinolines. In March 1937 *Vogue* became critical of the studios' preoccupation with bodice-rippers: 'A curious state of affairs now seems to exist in Hollywood. Everyone has gone into perpetual fancy-dress. There apparently isn't a female star out there who doesn't want to put on pantalettes, do her hair up in curls and a frizz, and go bouncing her hoops in front of the camera. There is such a thing as monotony.'

Surrealist ideals were used to launch an intellectual counter-attack. *Vogue*'s 'Eye View' of April 1937 was written below *Poeme Visible* by Max Ernst: 'This sums up our present state of mind. All eyes straining to probe what the couturiers are inventing to grace this season of seasons.' In July 1938 *Vogue* quoted Albert Einstein's theory of relativity – 'We're abandoning absolute time, too.'

In September 1937 *Vogue* voted Cole Porter's 'I've Got You Under My Skin' as the song of the year and used the phrase 'sex appeal' for the first time. Paris celebrated Ziegfeld Follies' glitter. This was a season of the sequin – 'They flash like a glance from a bright eye and kill their man at ten yards.' Sex was used to sell the New Look: 'There is a delicious excitement about these new clothes, for in them woman is re-discovering herself, her personality and her sex.'

In March 1938 *Vogue* heralded what it curiously called the 'Feminist movement in Paris' – opposite a wasp-waisted Winterhalter lady. The crinoline had landed. 'Obsolete adjectives come to mind, describing almost obsolete ideals. It is no longer so smart to be boyish. You must be the essence of romance at evening – you wear your satin corset outside your crinoline, pile your hair in a chignon topped with flowers, rustle forth in taffeta with lace petticoats.' *Vogue* cited key influences as the Renaissance, the seventeenth century, the 1880s, schooldays and childhood. On the brink of war, Paris snatched the director's chair – 'Paris backs the bustle', 'The case for slacks', 'Paris says you must have hips'. On 3 September 1939 the Second World War broke out. *Vogue* talked of restraint, common sense, warmth and rationing. Just as it was about to extol the virtues of wasp waists and fragility, Paris, with the brilliance of a seasoned acrobat, did a back flip.

1940–49

Home on leave. Be ready, then, to greet him. Now if ever, beauty is your duty. Now, if ever, by that crystal-clear conscience: clothes that will charm him. Remember – none but the fair deserve the brave.

The Return of the Soldier, *Vogue*, April 1940

SILK ON ITS LAST LEGS

WILL IT COME TO THIS?

With the world at war, London crumbling, and time bombs being dropped a stone's throw from its office, *Vogue* put its faith in fashion: 'It's pulse beats with imperishable vitality. As long as there is desire for change and love of self-expression, a sense of fitness and sense of fantasy – there will be fashion.' Before the outbreak of war, fashion was elitist and escapist. Now, clothes were part of the rallying cry for unity. The industry was frozen, fertile imaginations cut short. Sketchbooks were closed and fashion had metamorphosed into the unlikeliest of symbols: morale booster and government tool.

After decades of free reign and prolonged periods of decadence, the fashion industry had to be creative within the constraints of economic responsibility and social rules. The new words – austerity, rational and utility were delivered in Churchillian fashion; the concept of common sense was new. Women were in uniform and men were taken aback by this. In 1940 in a two-sided argument on the subject of women in uniform, Patrick Balfour talked about the downside as 'a sociological fallacy called feminine emancipation', followed by the ultimate insult: 'Hitler is very probably a woman. In figure, in stridency and in barbarous singleness of purpose, he is the equal of any Fräulein in uniform.'

Women were valiantly clinging to the last bastions of femininity. In 1941 *Vogue* pronounced that silk was on its last legs. Stockings were to be the sacrificial lamb of

LEFT **With 'Silk on its Last Legs', *Vogue* visualized the ultimate wartime insult: Fair Isle stockings worn to take tea at the Ritz, 1941.**

OPPOSITE **Actress Valerie Hobson, wearing a party dress by Rahvis, standing in the burnt remains of *Vogue*'s studio, November 1941.**

RIGHT **The 'Utility Collection',
featured in October 1942, was
British fashion's answer to
austerity – elegant, feminine
and using the minimum of
hard-wearing fabrics.**

RIGHT **The 'Utility Collection',
featured in October 1942, was
British fashion's answer to
austerity – elegant, feminine
and using the minimum of
hard-wearing fabrics.**

the fashion industry. 'Will it come to this?' said *Vogue*, pointing a
finger at a woman taking tea in a pair of frumpy Fair Isle stockings.
'The ban on silk stockings came as a great shock to feminine pride.
It is a great topic of feminine conversation. "What will we look
like?", "Thick wool legs in the Ritz?", "I can only bear sheer silk,"
"My dear, my ankles."'

While Britain was buckling down to austerity and clothing
coupons, America – alien to belt-tightening – provided the
glamour. *Vogue* trod the fine line between aspiration and reality,
reporting that American women are wearing 'a revolutionary new
silhouette with sloping shoulders … shirt-waist dresses. They
always wore them – they always will … dressed up with jewelled
buttons and a lyrical, hysterical hat.' On 1 June 1941 rationing of
cloth, clothing and footwear was introduced. Clothing requirements
had been reduced to 66 coupons. To add insult to injury, this was
the same quota as margarine.

In 1942 *Vogue* had already coined the phrase 'The New Look'
to describe the current state of mind. 'Dressiness is démodé. It
looks wrong to look wealthy. Understatement has a chic denied
to overemphasis.' Within the financial restraints, there was still
room for creativity. Propaganda prints were designed to get the
message over – 'Dig for Victory', 'Home Guard', 'Happy Landing'
and Vivien Leigh in a '66 coupons' design illustrated with rare
and rationed items. Necessity became the mother of invention.
'Clothes from Chemicals' was a new idea pioneered in America,
as a way of making tough materials which didn't deplete natural
resources – 'Nylon, a versatile chemical product which has
already been proved in hairbrushes, toothbrushes and the best-
wearing stockings in the world, is now being turned into soft,
woolly fleeces. These make coats with almost magic properties.'

In 1941 the British Government was desperately trying to
keep the fashion industry alive. The London Fashion Collection,
representing nine British designers including Norman Hartnell,
Edward Molyneux, Lachasse and Digby Morton toured Buenos
Aires, Montevideo, Rio de Janeiro and São Paulo. By 1942 the
British Government was forced to take direct action closer to
home, and leading designers Hartnell, Molyneux, Morton, Hardy
Amies, Victor Stiebel, Bianca Mosca and Peter Russell put their
heads together to come up with a Utility wardrobe.

As the war progressed, *Vogue*'s tone became increasingly
urgent and dictatorial: 'General Economy Issues his Orders of
the Day', ran next to a figurative collage of zips, stockings and
press studs. Saving paper for re-pulping, using up every scrap
of mending thread, hair pins and buttons, preserving zip
fasteners and re-covering old shoes was recommended.
Austerity extended to beauty treatments, too – 'Diluting just
the last bright drop of nail varnish for just one more application.
Gouging out the last crimson goodness from your lipstick.
Being sparing with face-powder and as cunning with face-
cream, working one tiny dollop into the danger spots under
the eyes, across the brow.'

In October 1942 fashion and politics were firm allies.
Austerity with a glamorous ingredient was called 'Fashionable
Intelligence' by *Vogue*: 'All the designs are, of course, within the
new austerity specification: only so many buttons, this much cuff
and that much skirt … but they are an object lesson in the power
of pure style over mere elegance.' Political implications of 'the
parcel-carrier and the pram-pusher, the government clerk and
the busy clerk' having access to the skills of London's couture
elite was described in socialist terms: 'It is a revolutionary
scheme and a heartening thought. It is, in fact, an outstanding
example of applied democracy.'

Because fabric had to be preserved at all costs, the emphasis
was firmly on accessories. But even here, economies had to be

ABOVE **Cecil Beaton's 'Fashion is Indestructible' shoot illustrated the fact that, even in the midst of bombing and destruction, fashion survives.**

made: 'Milliners must design hats that stay on without the benefit of elastic'; with straw in short supply, the summer alternative was a crocheted snood. Wooden-soled shoes save on the world shortage of leather. Shoulder bags were taking over – 'Big bags are best: they suit our mood for being self-sufficient.' With dye in short supply, colour was dull and practical. *Vogue* even suggested abandoning preconceived ideas about specific colours – 'You can make your black dress a seven-day-a-week-dress.' There were many ways of interchange to be considered, and buying came down to single items.

In September 1943 *Vogue* comprised a 'Portfolio of Wartime Economies' starting with 'Your One and Only Dress'. Cost-cutting measures became ever more ingenious as buying was edged out by recycling. In other words, shop hound makes do. Handbags were reconditioned with new lining and clasps, hats and clothes were remodelled, corsets reconditioned, stockings invisibly mended and shoes dyed.

In December 1943 *Vogue* featured two pin-up girls from the Ziegfeld Follies. In January 1944 the magazine presented a panorama of the past – 50 years of significant fashion changes,

'condensed almost to de-hydration point'. As the war neared its conclusion, *Vogue* wondered how the population would react when uniforms were exchanged for civilian dress. In September 1944 it speculated: 'Where is Fashion Going?' Designer Charles Creed predicted that dress restrictions would continue for a long time to come, C Willett Cunnington forecasted a craving for colour after five years of blackout and fashion historian James Laver speculated about a period of wild experiment. Only the British designer, Hardy Amies, had his finger on the button: 'From the scraps of refugee gossip and in illustrations in an odd fashion paper smuggled out, Paris shows us clothes which go just one step further in a perfectly logical sequence: minute waists, full billowing skirts set off by narrow shoulders. I believe in these new clothes – I feel them in my bones.'

When the American troops liberated Paris in 1944, former model and *Vogue* photographer Lee Miller reported from a city that was in raptures. 'Paris has gone mad ... The long, graceful, dignified avenues are crowded with flags and filled with screaming, cheering, pretty people. Everywhere in the streets were the dazzling girls, cycling, crawling up tank turrets. Their silhouette was very queer and fascinating to me after utility and austerity in England. Full floating skirts, tiny waist-lines. The entire gait of the French woman has changed with her footwear. Instead of the bounding buttocks and mincing steps of "pre-war", there is a hot-foot stride, picking up the whole foot at once.'

The following months were a tricky time for *Vogue*. Despite dangling a carrot with descriptions of Parisian chic, British austerity restrictions remained tighter than ever. *Vogue*'s strategy was to put elegance on a piece of elastic, then pull its readers back to reality. 'There is agitation against austerity,' wrote *Vogue* in November 1944. 'America's dress restrictions were only concerned with saving materials. Paris, as an occupied country, has had nothing of the kind. Already we are able to see one another's fashions. One day we shall be able to buy one another's fashions.'

In November 1944 Lee Miller described the first Paris couture collections since 1940 as being, 'simpler than those made under the occupation – plainer and more practical, but rich in ideas'. These included a quilted windbreaker by Marie-Louise Bruyère, Elsa Schiaparelli's fur culottes, Lucien Lelong's cocktail suit, appliquéd with jet-studded red leaves, and Mad Carpentier's apron basque. In December 1944 *Vogue* published its 'Paris Manifesto'. It was an attempt to placate its readers with a message from Lucien Lelong, president of the Chambre Syndicale de la Couture Parisienne, who categorically stated: 'Not more than forty models in any one collection. Not more than half the models to be in woollen materials, and the most important restriction: to limit yardage to 3 yards a dress, 4 yards a suit, 4⅔ yards a coat.'

The question of fashion leadership was hanging in the balance. Britain needed to compete on the world stage if it was to survive. 'It is a vital question,' observed *Vogue* in May 1945, 'for on it hangs great affairs of

VOGUE

THE LONDON COLLECTIONS AND SPRING FABRICS
INCLUDING VOGUE PATTERN BOOK   THE CONDÉ NAST PUBLICATIONS LTD.   MARCH, 1948 · PRICE 3/-

national and international trade, employment and standards of living.' Although British *Vogue* had always actively supported London designers, the war signalled the beginning of an international attitude to fashion. In July *Vogue* printed the first Soviet State Fashion Show report, radioed in from Moscow. *Vogue*'s October 1945 issue was entitled 'Peace and Reconstruction' and had a cloudless sky on the cover. Inside, *Vogue* dovetailed the new demobilization wardrobe and reported on Elsa Schiaparelli's return to Paris when, after a four-year absence, 'the cry, "La patronne, la patronne," ran through the house like a tongue of flame'.

The following year, October 1946, *Vogue* reported that 'Paris revels in femininity' and described the 'Britain Can Make It' exhibition, which had taken place at the Victoria and Albert Museum on 24 September. In January 1947 *Vogue* defined America's new age group, which was to dominate market forces in the 1950s, stating in 'Truth about the Teen-ager': 'They are no less human than their parents and, though their fashions may be cut alike, their philosophies are not.'

In April 1947 *Vogue* witnessed the most extreme shift in fashion since 1910. With his new collection, Christian Dior had

become the new name in Paris. A wit dubbed his collection, 'the Battle of the Marne of the couture'. Pronouncing his ideas as 'fresh and put over with great authority', *Vogue* described the details of his revolutionary New Look – his 'wide waistband and, whittling the waist, the deeply, widely cut bodice'. Cue the hard-hitting punch line: 'Dior uses fabric lavishly in skirts – fifteen yards in a woollen day dress, twenty-five yards in a short taffeta evening dress.'

Launched in an atmosphere of austerity and oppression, the general consensus on the collection was one of moral outrage. *Vogue*, however, unanimously voted it a feat of unparalleled perfection, gasping at the proportional representation of wasp waists, full skirts, narrow shoulders and wide hats. In October of that year, *Vogue* looked even more closely. The sinuous silhouette could not be created with flesh and fabric alone. Dior's corset had a taffeta underbodice with rose ruffles at the breasts and a ruffled hip. Not content with throwing the perfect curve, he had ingeniously designed an understructure of the feminine ideal. The magazine ominously announced, 'There are moments when fashion changes fundamentally. When it is more than a matter of differences in detail. The whole fashion attitude seems to change – the whole structure of the body. This is one of those moments.'

With the hourglass silhouette firmly fixed in female consciousness, fashion entered an experimental phase. Fabric – and copious quantities of it – was flying in all directions. There were back-dipping skirts, uneven hemlines and peplums standing to attention. In October 1948 *Vogue* reported a 'wing-back décolleté of the Dior dress. Huge flapping cuffs like seals' fins'.

The following year, *Vogue* cut to 'the details that spike the Paris collection', outlining the 'gamine haircut, deep décolletages, starched Eton collars on dinner suits. Pockets like croissants. Buttons, buttons, buttons', and endless asymmetry. With the publication of a picture of the Countess Alain de la Falaise wearing Jeanne Paquin's cut velvet and taffeta, the future was assured. *Vogue* wrote: 'There is news of beautifully designed, desirable clothes with the fixed purpose of interesting, of dramatizing a woman.'

OPPOSITE Cristobal Balenciaga – the undisputed master of construction. His 'grand ballgown of great dignity' was shot in his salon against a painting of Versailles.

RIGHT Christian Dior's sublime cocktail dress of 1949 featured a nipped-in waist and spiralling skirt – the 1950s look of total elegance and grooming had already evolved.

INDEX

PICTURE CREDITS

The publishers would like to thank the following sources and The Condé Nast Publications for their kind permission to reproduce the pictures in this book:

t: top, b: bottom, l: left, r: right, tl: top left, tr: top right, bl: bottom left, br: bottom right, bc: bottom centre, bcl: bottom centre left, bcr: bottom centre right.

All images © *Vogue*, The Condé Nast Publications Ltd.

American Press Association 20b
Antonio 154l
Tony Armstrong-Jones 46
Michel Arnaud 185, 195, 196, 217, 249
Clive Arrowsmith 63, 245, 253bcr

David Bailey 10bl, 55, 57br,tl, 61, 64b, 146t, 151, 215
Cecil Beaton 10cl, 34tr, 37, 38, 39, 40, 41, 156, 160–1, 223tr,bl
Maurice Beck & Helen Macgregor 27t, 138, 207tl
Edouard Benito 11cl, 26tr, 36
Christian Bérard 35, 177, 180
Bettmann/Corbis (jacket)
Eric Boman 67, 98, 178, 222
René Bouché 8, 49tr, 51t, 96, 112
Brad Branson 243

Regan Cameron 170, 184
Pierre Cardin 107
Oleg Cassini 108
Castaldi 139
Alex Chatelain 72, 74, 87tl, 99, 103, 130, 132, 252br
Willie Christie 97, 166-7
Henry Clarke 49bl, 52, 53, 56, 95, 125, 211, 149, 211, 250obr
Clifford Coffin 7, 10c, 42tr, 43t,b, 44, 126

Corinne Day 9, 81
John Deakin 48
Patrick Demarchelier 73b, 75, 76, 80t, 87tr, 89, 175, 181, 218, 233, 253bcl
Anthony Denney 50, 256
Terence Donovan Archive 82, 229
Helen Dryden 10tl, 25
Brian Duffy 212

Rodger Duncan 240

Arthur Elgort 62, 73t, 83, 91, 159tl, 179, 242
Perry Ellis 131
Robert Erdmann 153, 172, 225
Carl Erickson 32tl, 34l, 42tl, 93, 204, 238
Lee Creelman Erickson 182

Hans Feurer 54, 92
Ann Fish 11cr, 29t

Oberto Gili 79
Ruth Sigrid Grafstrom 32b
Mats Gustaffson 146br

Michel Haddi 190, 252bl
Will Hammell 19
Anna Harvey 247
Don Honeyman 87bl, 173tl

Paul Iribe 17

Just Jaeckin 59
Mikael Jansson 110, 246

Donna Karan 164
Neil Kirk 122
Kelly Klein 105
Nick Knight 9, 86cr, 152, 174
Kim Knott 86tc, 124, 143
Eddy Kohli 86cl, 191

Andrew Lamb 80b, 84b, 87c, 158, 159br, 176, 192, 197, 230, 234, 235
Barry Lategan 64t, 66c, 69, 208, 248, 251br
Bruce Laurence 154r
Roger Law 58
Peter Lindbergh 77, 78, 128, 253bl

Andrew Macpherson 142, 236, 251bcr, 252bcl
Eamonn J McCabe 171
Frances McLaughlin-Gill 51b, 94
André Marty 31
Herbert Matter 86br, 134
Raymond Meier 102, 148, 254
Sheila Metzner 165
Baron Adolphe De Meyer 22br
David Montgomery 114, 115tl,br, 162, 251bcl

Tom Munro 85, 116, 186, 189, 209, 220, 237

Helmut Newton 109

Jacques Olivar 1, 3, 201, 241

Pablo & Delia 66
Norman Parkinson 90, 198
Penati 147tl, 251bl
Irving Penn 47
Douglas Pollard 27b, 188, 239
Antony Price 210

John Rawlings 183
Herb Ritts 71
Robert 11tr, 65
Richard Rutledge 45

St John 13
Yves Saint Laurent 219
Lothar Schmid 68, 199
David Sims 11br, 84t
Lord Snowdon 70
Bert Stern 200

Mario Testino 4–5, 87cr,bl, 113, 127, 145, 169, 231
Ronald Traeger 10br, 6otl,tr,b, 213

Valentino 232
Javier Vallhonrat 86tr,tl,bc, 135, 141, 163, 221
Marcel Vertès 6, 33
Justin de Villeneuve 100, 101
Tony Viramontes 144

Albert Watson 104, 155, 226, 253br
Martin Welch 202
Porter Woodruff 244, 250obcr

Every effort has been made to acknowledge correctly and contact the source and/copyright holder of each picture, and Carlton Books Limited apologizes for any unintentional errors or omissions which will be corrected in future editions of this book.

ACKNOWLEDGEMENTS

Very special thanks to Erika Frei for her encouragement
and advice on the fine art of tact and diplomacy.
To Joyce Douglas for being there.

Thank you to *Vogue's* superb library staff
– Darlene Maxwell, Chris Pipe, Nancy Kim, headed by
the brilliant Lisa Hodgkins – for their support, good humour
and company throughout this project.

Two people who were fundamental: endless thanks
to Francesca Harrison, picture editor, for being calm,
efficient and having a lovely eye. Emily Wheeler-Bennett,
Condé Nast's editorial business and rights director,
for being a complete professional and friend.

This book is dedicated to my mother, father and
brother Billy with love.